CONTENTS

INTRODUCTION

The first bike was made in France in the 1690s. It was merely a wooden beam with wheels fixed on it. The cyclist would sit on a cushion and steer with their feet. Biking has come a long way since then.

Important developments

Since the 17th century there have been considerable changes. Here are some of the important dates and the changes which were made:

1791 –	an early type of bike known as the **celerifere** was exhibited at the Palais Royale in Paris. It was a wooden beam with wheels.
1816 –	the first two-wheeled bike with steering was made in Germany. The first ones used in England were known as **hobby horses**. Two years later a slightly better version, called the **dandy horse**, was developed.
1839 –	a Scottish blacksmith, Kirkpatrick Macmillan, added the first driving levers and pedals.
1855 –	the **velocipede** was made in France. It had a wooden frame and wheels; iron tyres were attached to the front wheel.
1869 –	solid rubber tyres were added and the name 'bicycle' was used for the first time.
1880 –	the first bike was produced with front and rear wheels of the same size, pedals with **sprockets**, and **gears** and chains. It also used ball bearings for smooth running and pneumatic (inflated) tyres for a more comfortable ride.

These early bikes had no pedals or brakes and were just pushed along with the feet.

Cheap and efficient!

Greater interest in cycling began in the 1960s and 70s mainly due to people's increased awareness of environmental factors. Cycling was a cheap, efficient and environmentally-friendly way of getting about!

It was in 1977 in the United States that the first, basic **all-terrain bikes (ATBs)** were developed. They had reinforced frames, knobbly tyres for improved grip and racing-bike gears.

This early Specialized stunt jumper shows the strong frame and large tyres which make a mountain bike.

In 1980 an American company called 'Specialized' put out the first mass-produced mountain bike. At the same time some Japanese companies, such as Suntour, were making the first special components for mountain bikes.

Since 1980 progress and developments have been very rapid. Mountain bike cross-country racing became an Olympic event for the first time in Atlanta, USA in 1996.

5

WHAT IS A MOUNTAIN BIKE?

Tough, chunky, rugged and durable are all words that describe the modern mountain bike. A mountain bike is designed for strength, versatility and speed. It's ideal for hard workouts on tough terrain which is why it is often referred to as an **all-terrain bike**.

Saddle and seat post

Some mountain bikes have seats with quick releases to allow for easy adjustment. To find the right setting push one pedal down as low as it will go, so that the **pedal cranks** are vertical. If you are seated with your instep in the lowest pedal your leg should be just slightly bent.

The latest **suspension systems** on saddles make riding more comfortable.

Transmission and gearing system

The transmission includes the pedals, pedal crank set, chain and the cogs on the rear wheel. These parts convert the power from your pedalling legs into the movement of the bike's rear wheel.

Most mountain bikes have 15 to 27 gears. The gearing system consists of the front and rear **derailleur**, the rear **sprockets** and the **gear** levers. The rider chooses the most appropriate gear for the terrain using the gear levers on the handlebars. A wide choice of gears makes cycling easier, both up and downhill.

Frame

The frame is usually made from either steel or **alloy** tubing which is strong yet relatively light. Recently, new materials such as titanium and carbon fibre have been used and these reduce the weight of the bike even more, making the bikes easier to manoeuvre and pedal uphill. In recent years there has also been the addition of front and rear suspension to some models.

Steering system

This comprises the front fork, handlebars, handlebar stem and the bearings of the headset. A strong and durable system gives you better steering precision. Extensions are available that bolt onto the end of your handlebars to allow for extra riding positions.

Brakes

There are front and rear brakes which, when well-adjusted, allow you to slow down with fingertip control. **Cantilever brakes** (also called V brakes) are the most common type.

Wheels

Modern wheels are both light and strong. They are made with narrow aluminium rims that are light and very flexible. Chunky tyres with good grips are fitted back and front, often with quick-release **hubs**. You can also get carbon rims that are even lighter and stronger, but also more expensive!

THE BiKE FOR YOU

There is a very wide range of mountain bikes so you have to make sure that you get the best bike for you. Here are some basic tips.

Requirements

What sort of riding do you need your bike for? If you are a beginner then an all-round bike would be best. If you are going to try a lot of off-road riding or even racing then you will need a specialized bike. Most of the manufacturers make special children's bikes and these can be fully adjusted – you can even get small adults' bikes. One of these types would probably be the best to start with.

Cost

You can pay any amount of money up to over £1000 for a top-of-the-range bike! When budgeting don't forget to include the cost of a helmet, lock, lights and other essential equipment.

Size

Your bike must be the right size for you. Bikes have different frame sizes and different wheel sizes and both of these will affect the overall size of the bike. One simple test is to stand astride the bike with your feet flat on the floor. If the bike size is correct you should have a gap of about 8 cm between your backside and the top of the frame.

You must get the right size bike frame. You can adjust the height to fit.

At the shop

Compare all of the prices of the bikes on offer and make sure they have all that you want, such as the number of **gears** and type of tyres.

Always have a test ride so that you can check that the size is right, that the bike feels comfortable and that the brakes work properly. When you buy from a shop you should always ask for a free first service, so that you can take the bike back for a check up after you have ridden it.

If you can, get your bike from a specialized shop. When you get there you may be confused by the amount of choice, so go prepared!

SAFETY FIRST

🚲 Before buying a bike check that it is legal and **roadworthy**. Check especially that a second-hand bike has reasonable treads on the tyres and the brakes work properly.

WHAT GEAR DO YOU NEED?

Before you go out on your mountain bike you need to think carefully about what you need to wear – and what you need to take with you. There is nothing to stop you from wearing your own normal leisure clothing. However, avoid anything loose-fitting that could get caught in the wheels or chains. For real comfort and added safety the right kit is essential.

Helmet

An essential piece of equipment which you really must get into the habit of wearing every time you get on your bike! There are lots of modern, colourful designs with very stylish looks. Make sure you get one that fits properly. It should fit low on your head (but not obstruct your vision) and snugly so that it does not wobble from side to side. Get the best quality helmet you can afford, try a few on and ask for some expert advice.

Arms and upper body

You should wear a long-sleeved top that perhaps has some built-in padding. It is also a good idea to wear elbow pads over the top, too.

Gloves

You should wear gloves. Many cycling mitts are padded for comfort but you really need some tough full-fingered gloves that will give you full protection.

Cycling shorts

You can buy padded lycra cycling shorts (much more comfortable on that hard saddle!) and as long as you wear them without underwear and wash them after every trip they are the best way to avoid any soreness.

PROTECTION FROM PAIN

🚲 You need to protect any parts of your body that you can – you will be riding over rough territory and falling off can be painful!

Sunglasses

For perfect vision and complete eye protection you should buy a good pair of sunglasses with lenses that can be changed depending on the weather conditions.

Legs

For rough terrain your legs should be covered with a stout pair of trousers – jeans are quite good for this as they are made from strong material. You can buy special trousers and you might like to add some knee pads as well for extra protection!

Shoes

You could wear just ordinary trainers but you can also buy specialist pedal/shoe combinations of various types that have a stiff shoe-sole with a cleat system – a system that easily attaches and detaches your shoe from the pedal.

KEEPING FIT AND HEALTHY

Riding a bike is physically demanding and it can be quite hard work. You will need to have a good level of general fitness. Cycling itself is one of the best ways to get fit!

Warm-up

Before each riding session you should **warm-up** to get your body properly prepared for what is to come. It's a good idea to perform some stretching exercises on various parts of your body as these can prevent injuries. In your warm-up try to stretch out and mobilize all the body areas you will be using when riding. All of these exercises are just examples.

Quadricep stretch

Bend one knee and pull your foot up behind you. Hold this for 10 seconds then do the other leg. ....

Cool-down

When you are on your bike you are in a fairly fixed position and you might find that you are very stiff when you get off. It's for this reason that you should cool-down when you finish. You should repeat your warm-up but not for so long. This gives your body a chance to recover.

Neck stretch ·····························

Gently pull your head towards your shoulders. Hold for 10 seconds then do the other side.

Hamstring stretch

Sit as shown and reach for your toes keeping your head down. Hold for 10 seconds. Repeat six times for each leg.

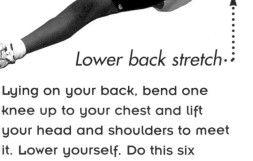

Lower back stretch·

Lying on your back, bend one knee up to your chest and lift your head and shoulders to meet it. Lower yourself. Do this six times before doing the other side.

The right food

If you are going to be doing a lot of riding check that you are eating the correct foods. If you go out on a ride that might be for well over an hour, take some food along to eat.

Items you should consider taking along:

- Bananas – these are high in carbohydrates which give energy

- Dried fruit – these are also good energy foods

- Energy bars – there are all sorts of these available

- Water – this is essential to stop you from **dehydrating**

The main advantage of all of these is that they are easy and light to carry. You can fit a water bottle to the frame of your bike so that you can take drinks as you are riding along. Try to drink at least a bottle of water every hour, more in hot weather.

BEFORE YOU SET OFF

Mountain biking is a dangerous sport and can lead to injury. There is a chance that you could crash off your bike and be lying injured in a very inaccessible spot. You should never ride alone in a remote area.

Prepare for the worst

If you do decide to go by yourself on an on-and-off-the-road ride make sure that you leave details behind about where you are going and how long you expect to be gone. If you have an accident someone will at least know where you are and can get help to you.

Pre-ride checks

Before you go off on your bike there are some other safety checks you should do:

- Make sure that you have enough time to complete your planned route in daylight! You don't want to be off-road in the dark!
- Check the weather forecast. Severe weather can also cause you problems, especially in hilly areas.

BE SEEN!

🚲 If the light is poor make sure you wear bright clothing and some reflective strips or a harness. Even in sunlight bright clothing is advisable so that motorists can spot you with ease.

Before you set off make sure that you are wearing the correct safety equipment and that your bike is in a **roadworthy** condition.

What to pack

As well as your food there are some other items you might like to take:

- plenty of water to drink so that there is no danger of becoming **dehydrated**.

- basic spares and tools for your bike, such as a **puncture** repair kit.

- sunscreen – it is very easy to get sunburnt on a bike, and sunburn can be very painful!

- insect repellent – this may be essential in some areas.

- money – you should take enough to cover possible transport home and at least enough for an emergency telephone call!

▲ Puncture repair kit

Sunscreen

Insect repellent

SAFETY FIRST

🚲 Remember to put on all the necessary protective clothing. Don't forget that helmet – it could save your life!

TOWN BIKING

Checklist

The first place you are likely to ride your bike is around town. There are a few things you should check before you do this.

1 Are you confident on your bike, well-balanced on the saddle and unlikely to topple over? Is your balance good enough for you to be able to look from side to side with confidence?

2 Do you know the rules of the road or the 'Highway Code'? If not, then you need to learn. You can join a local club that will teach you all the basics, such as the correct hand signals.

Steering

An essential skill is steering. At low speeds you must turn your handlebars to steer. As you turn a corner or bend, the bike will lean, so allow your body to lean with it. For **high-speed turns** the bike will lean with you naturally and take you round a corner – you will only have to use the handlebars a little.

You will need to be able to lean your bike into corners as you go round them.

Gear changing

Your mountain bike will have a lot of **gears** and you need to get used to changing them and selecting the right gears. The lower the gear, the easier it is to pedal, so you need a low gear to go uphill and a high gear for flat areas and downhill. Try to ride in the gear that is most comfortable for you.

You should not have to strain too hard or stand up in the saddle – when it's hard work, change down a gear.

You should always try to change gear when you are not pushing too hard on the pedals, so try to ease off before each gear change. Try out all of the gears on your bike and practise changing from one to another until you can do it smoothly and safely.

Braking

You have both a front and rear brake on your bike so make sure you know which is which! If you pull on your front brake too quickly you can be forced forward over the handlebars or the front tyre may lose its grip. Always try to slow down by squeezing both brakes together smoothly and gently, and then apply more force.

You should not go on to any other form of riding until you have mastered all the skills mentioned!

Remember, you don't have to put your brakes fully on or fully off – you can gently apply your brakes just to slow down.

SAFETY FIRST
🚲 Always try to slow down gradually and avoid **emergency braking**.

OFF-ROAD SKILLS

You will have learned that to stay in balance while turning corners you must move your body weight. When you try out the following skills this is equally important.

Going downhill

Going downhill or **descending** is one of the most exciting parts of riding your mountain bike. However, you will be travelling at the highest speeds and the chances of an accident are greater.

Keep your weight back as far over the rear wheel as you can and start to apply your brakes (this is known as **feathering**). You might need to stand up slightly on the pedals so that your legs act like a **suspension system**. Keep feathering your brakes but keep your hands wide on the handlebars to get maximum control.

Going downhill in areas such as this requires practice and skillful riding.

SAFETY FIRST

🚲 Start off with a gentle slope and make sure you can cope with that before you go on to really steep ones!

Going uphill

Climbing or **ascending** can be very hard work and all the **gears** you have on your mountain bike will be very useful.

Before you start climbing a hill or slope make sure that you have selected the right gear. It's easier to change down before you get to the really steep bits rather than wait until you are on them. Try to keep your weight forward and quite low. Stay sitting in the saddle. This way you get a better grip or **traction** and it will give you more power to get up the hill.

Remember to keep looking ahead of you to find the easiest route up, avoiding any obstacles that might be in your way!

Cornering

You will corner much slower than usual if you are going uphill and much faster if you are going downhill, so you have to know what to do!

The basic rules of cornering are that you should always brake before you are at the corner. You must also lean into the corner while extending your outside leg to balance your weight.

You might have to do a **low-speed turn** if you are ascending and you should be able to do a tight turn. If you are descending on a **high-speed turn** you need to take as wide a turn as you can.

SAFETY FIRST

🚲 You never know what might be around a tight corner – another rider, or walker perhaps. So always be ready to brake and stop if necessary.

DEALING WITH OBSTACLES

When you are off-road you will come across many obstacles. One of the best things about having your mountain bike is that you may be able to go over them if your learn the right techniques!

Front wheel lift

The most basic technique is the **front wheel lift**, which you can use to get up and over a kerb and logs.

A front wheel lift needs a good deal of practice. You need to try this with very small and low obstacles at first and work your way up to the more difficult ones!

Keep the bike in a low **gear**, slide your weight back and bend down with your elbows low. Push down with your strongest leg with its pedal high and then lift the handlebars up at the same time, moving your weight back. This should lift the front wheel up off the ground.

SAFETY FIRST

- 🚲 Remember that at all times you must be wearing all the proper safety equipment!

- 🚲 Never ride over an edge or slope without knowing the height of the drop first!

Bunny hop

There may be times when you and your bike have to take off completely. This manoeuvre is known as a bunny hop. This is not as difficult as it looks – and it's great fun!

Try it on some level, soft grass at first. Pedal along and decide where you want to jump. Before you get there bend down over the bike with your weight low. When you want to jump, spring your body up and lift up the handlebars at the same time. As soon as the front wheel starts to lift pull up your legs and feet so that the rear wheel lifts as well. Don't forget that you will be coming down as well! Relax your arms and legs and allow them to absorb your landing. Try to level the bike out so that both wheels land at the same time.

Doing jumps on your bike can be fun but requires a lot of practice.

Dropping off

You might find that you take off quite often, especially if you are riding quite fast towards steep edges or slopes. Going over these in the air is known as dropping off. Keep your pedals level, lift the front wheel off as you go over the edge and then use the same techniques for the landing as you did with your bunny hop. You might be coming down from a bit of a height, so make sure you really relax your arms and legs as you land!

Dropping off is an advanced skill that you should only do in areas you have checked first.

DEALING WITH DIFFERENT TERRAINS

One of the best things about mountain biking is being able to go over different types of terrain which you might not normally travel over. Each will require slightly different skills.

Mud

You can just about guarantee that you will have to ride through mud. Be very careful that you don't get stuck in deep mud and wherever possible, try to go around particularly muddy areas.

Leaning back and lifting the front wheel allows the back wheel to grip and helps you cycle through muddy areas.

As you approach a muddy area make sure that you are in a low **gear** and keep your weight back in the saddle and towards the rear of the bike. Try to keep pedalling right through the mud – if you stop you are likely to become stuck. The drive is coming from your rear wheel so try to keep the front wheel up and your weight back until you come out of the mud. You can then transfer your weight forward for the front wheel to grip onto the firmer ground.

Water

You may come across a puddle or even a stream or river. Always make sure that you do not enter water that is too deep – if it comes up above the level of the centre **hub** of your wheels you should not be riding into it.

TOP TIPS

- 🚲 When planning your route always check that you are allowed to cycle in the areas you choose.

- 🚲 Be sensitive to the environment – mountain bikes can destroy wild flowers and damage grasslands.

When you ride through water you should make sure that you are in a low gear and that you reduce your speed. Go into the water slowly, lifting your front wheel slightly as you do so and continue to pedal. Increase your speed as you come out of the water, but be careful as your tyres will be wet and slippery. Also remember that your wheels will be wet and this will reduce the efficiency of your brakes!

SAFETY FIRST

🚲 Never enter water if you are not sure how deep it is!

Always check your brakes after riding through water. Testing them helps to dry them off.

Gravel and sand

These materials are loose and difficult to ride through. Sand can be very tiring as it's difficult to get a good grip on it. Use a low gear in these conditions and grip your handlebars tightly so that you are not thrown off line. With gravel or loose stones you also have to be careful of stones or chips flying up towards you or other riders. Always keep your distance from other cyclists as they pass through gravel or you may be hit by grit flying up from their rear tyres!

Hold tight and concentrate when riding through loose, rough materials – they always wobble your steering.

TAKING IT FURTHER

Now that you have practised the skills of mountain biking, you may want to take it further. If you want to ride more seriously or competitively, there are many local clubs that organize the following events.

Cross-country

These events usually take place on a marked out loop track, with circuits from 1 to 10 kilometres long. Usually everyone starts together – with the fastest riders at the front. The circuit often involves hills, descents and flat parts. The winner is usually the fastest rider.

Crossing water is all part of the challenge of a cross-country race.

Trailquest

Trailquests vary but they are generally similar to an orienteering course using your bike. You have to go to certain points using a map, collect information, visit checkpoints and get back to the start point within given times.

Many of these events are organized for older, more experienced riders and one of them, the Polaris Challenge, even has an overnight stop. This means that the competitors have to take full camping equipment and food along as well – a real challenge!

Downhill

This is becoming more and more popular. It is a type of **time trial**, which means that each rider gets one chance to ride down the course and the fastest time is the winner! You must have all the correct protective equipment on if you are going to try this!

Dual slalom

This is like a **downhill** event but two riders have to ride down a course swerving in and out and around poles, often making jumps as well! This is usually a knockout competition that ends with the best two riders riding in the final.

Downhill is a timed event and you have to get down as quickly as possible.

These two cyclists are competing against each other in this dual slalom.

Your bike will need looking after carefully if it's to give you good service and perform properly and safely. If you have a major problem with it you will need to take it to a shop or dealer to get it fixed but there are quite a few things you can do yourself.

General checks

Before you go out on your bike you should spend a few minutes checking its basic components. If you do find a problem get it fixed! You don't want to be far away and find that you have to walk back because you didn't check something properly. You should have a **manual** with your bike and this will give you full details on what to check and what you can adjust for yourself.

Brakes

The **brake blocks** or pads will wear down because they are designed to rub against the rim of the wheel. Check that they are in the right position (level with the wheels) and that they have not worn down too much. Adjusting them and replacing them is very easy, and only takes a couple of minutes – time very well spent!

You should also regularly check the brake cables for any sign of damage, especially fraying. Some bikes have a **cable adjuster** on the brake levers. If the brake cables are getting loose with wear, you can use the cable adjusters to tighten them.

Wheels and tyres

Your tyres are in contact with the ground all the time you are riding so they are bound to get worn. The most annoying thing to get is a **puncture** so check for wear and look out for any thorns or pieces of glass or wire on your tyres.

You should always keep your tyres well-pumped up and make sure that the tread has not worn down. When they do wear down get some new ones!

Cleaning and oiling

Your bike is going to get very dirty if you are riding off-road and will need cleaning when you get home. You can wash it or hose it down to get most of the mud and dirt off and then you should oil or grease the moving parts (your manual will tell you about this).

The chainset, **gears** and pedals need **lubricating** regularly and they may also need some minor adjustments such as tightening up nuts and bolts. These are some of the more complicated parts of your bike so you may want to ask an expert to check them for you.

Remember that there are parts of your bike that will wear out and need replacing – you have to be prepared for this. Also, for your safety, and comfort, you should check it carefully and regularly, especially before riding and when you get back.

SAFETY FIRST

🚲 If you have any doubts about the safety or maintenance of your bike always take it to a specialist shop or mechanic so that it can be thoroughly checked.

Mountain biking is quite a new sport. The first competitive races were in Marin County, California, USA, in the 1980s.

The first championships

The first World Championships were held in Purgatory, Colorado, USA, in 1990. The first Mountain Biking World Cup Series took place in 1991, involving the two continents of Europe and North America. At that time there was only cross-country racing and it was not until 1993 that a six-event **Downhill** World Cup was added.

Word Cup Series

The World Cup Series involves riders from Europe and the United States and takes place over about eight months in different countries.

The events can be on any type of course, from alpine mountains to city parks, and each race lasts from about 1 hour 45 minutes to 2 hours.

One of the most successful of the early riders was Henrick Djernis from Denmark who in 1994 won the World Championship for the third time in a row!

Downhill events

These are some of the most popular international events and are especially popular with the television networks. There is usually a limit of about 140 riders for the actual race. If more enter, qualifying events select the fastest 90 who go into the semi-finals against the top 50 riders in the world standings. These races are becoming more and more difficult and dangerous, and riders now wear full **body armour** and **full-faced helmets**.

World Championships

The most important event is the World Championships – this is the one that all riders want to win. It is held every year in a different country and it takes place over ten days.

The course is selected very carefully and includes long sections of technical single track, a climb at altitude, technical fast downhills and a variety of different surfaces. The top riders who take part in all of these types of events are professionals and take their training and racing very seriously.

Downhill events are competed over very challenging courses and at great speeds.

Shaun Palmer in the downhill race of the 1997 World Championships.

GLOSSARY

alloy a metal mixed with one or more other elements

all-terrain bikes (ATB) another term for mountain bikes

ascending going uphill

body armour protective clothing worn by downhill racers

brake block the part of the brake that is in contact with the wheel rim

cable adjuster a brake adjuster found in the brake levers

Cantilever brake a brake that moves on a pivot in order to exert pressure on either side of a wheel's rim

celerifere an early design of a bike

dandy horse an early design of a bike

dehydrating when the body lacks or has a shortage of fluids such as water

derailleur a bike gear which works by changing the line of the chain while pedalling so that it jumps to a different sprocket

descending going downhill

downhill a specific event where riders race on a downhill course

emergency braking pulling on the brakes very hard and quickly

feathering gently pulling the brake on and off to control speed

front wheel lift lifting the front wheel up off the ground over an obstacle

full-faced helmet a safety helmet that covers the whole face and head of a rider

gears a mechanism of moving parts that can transmit or regulate motion

high-speed turn cornering very fast, usually on a downhill course

hobby horse an early design of a bike

hub the central part of a wheel

low-speed turn cornering at low speed, usually when on an uphill course

lubricating greasing or oiling various parts of your bike as necessary

manual an instruction booklet that comes with each bike and gives detailed information about it

pedal crank the arm that joins a pedal to the bottom bracket on a bike

puncture a damaged tyre, usually causing it to go flat

roadworthy a bike that is in good condition overall and suitable to ride

sprocket a cog on a bike, such as those driven by the chain

suspension systems the spring and shock absorbers used to absorb jolting and protect the bike from damage

time trial a road race in which the winner makes the fastest time

traction the amount of grip a tyre has on the ground

velocipede an early design of a bike

warm-up a series of stretching exercises you should perform before riding to prepare your body

USEFUL ADDRESSES

With over 1,100 clubs in the UK, the British Cycling Federation can put you in touch with cyclists throughout the country. They can also advise you on where and when to ride and publish a calendar of events.

British Cycling Federation
National Cycling Centre
Stuart Street
Manchester
M11 4DQ
Telephone: 0161 230 2301
Fax: 0161 231 0591

Union Cycliste Internationale (UCI) -
International Cycling Union
37 Route de Chavannes
Case Postale
CH 1000 Lausanne 23
Suisse
Tel: 21 622 0580
Fax: 21 622 0588

National Cycling Network
Tel: 01179 290888

Forest Enterprise
0131 3145322

British Waterways
01923 226422

British Schools Cycling Association
21 Bedhampton Road
North End
Portsmouth
PO2 7JX
Tel: 01705 642226
Fax: 01705 660187

Bushrangers MTB Club Sunshine Coast
Inc
PO Box 5646
Maroochydore
Queensland 4558
Australia

FURTHER READING

Books

Know the game: Mountain Biking, Brant Richards, A&C Black

Learn Mountain Biking in a Weekend, Andy Bull, Dorling Kindersley

The Complete Book of Mountainbiking, Brant Richards, Colins Willow

Magazines

Cycling and Mountain Biking Today, Cycling Today Ltd

Mountain Biker International, Link House Magazines

Websites

www.bcf.uk.com

www.sustrans.org.uk

www.greatoutdoors.com/imba

INDEX

796.6

Kirk Bizley

Heinemann
LIBRARY

www.heinemann.co.uk
Visit our website to find out more information about **Heinemann Library** books.

To order:
- ☎ Phone 44 (0) 1865 888066
- 🖹 Send a fax to 44 (0) 1865 314091
- 💻 Visit the Heinemann Bookshop at www.heinemann.co.uk to browse our catalogue and order online.

First published in Great Britain by Heinemann Library, Halley Court, Jordan Hill, Oxford OX2 8EJ, a division of Reed Educational and Professional Publishing Ltd.

Heinemann is a registered trademark of Reed Educational & Professional Publishing Limited.

OXFORD   MELBOURNE   AUCKLAND
JOHANNESBURG   BLANTYRE   GABORONE
IBADAN   PORTSMOUTH NH (USA)   CHICAGO

Designed by Celia Floyd
Originated by HBM Print Ltd, Singapore
Printed in Hong Kong by Wing King Tong

ISBN 0 431 03676 4 (hardback)
04 03 02 01 00
10 9 8 7 6 5 4 3 2 1

ISBN 0 431 03685 3 (paperback)
04 03 02 01 00
10 9 8 7 6 5 4 3 2 1

British Library Cataloguing in Publication Data

Bizley, Kirk
   Mountain Biking. – (Radical sports)
   1. All terrain cycling – Juvenile literature
   I. Title
   796.6'3

Acknowledgements

The Publishers would like to thank the following for permission to reproduce photographs:

Mary Evans Picture Library, p. 4; Chris Honeywell, pp. 10-11, 13, 15; Stockfile, pp. 6, 8, 9, 12, 16-28 (Steven Behr), pp.5 bottom, 29 bottom (Malcolm Fearon), p. 29 top (Jim McRoy).

Cover photograph reproduced with permission of Action Plus/NealHaynes

Our thanks to Bruce Johnson of the British Cycling Federation for his comments in the preparation of this book.

Every effort has been made to contact copyright holders of any material reproduced in this book. Any omissions will be rectified in subsequent printings if notice is given to the Publisher.

Any words appearing in the text in bold, **like this**, are explained in the Glossary.

This book aims to cover all the essential techniques of this radical sport but it is important when learning a new sport to get expert tuition and to follow any manufacturers' instructions.